Ultimate Bitcoin For Beginners Guide!

Bitcoin

I0503224

Be Part Of The Currency Revolution And Understand Bitcoin Market Basics, Mining, Trading, Cryptocurrency, And More!

James Harper

STOP!!! Before you read any further....Would you like to know the Secrets of Transforming your life, overcome insecurities, develop leadership skills, and undeniable confidence in your personal, professional, and relationship life?

If your answer is yes, then you are not alone. Thousands of people are looking for the secret to have unstoppable confidence and self-driven power in all areas of their lives.

If you have been searching for these answers without much luck, you're in the right place!

Not only will you gain incredible insight in this book, but because I want to make sure to give you as much value as possible, right now for a limited time you can get full **100% FREE access to a VIP bonus EBook** entitled **LIMITLESS ENERGY!**

Just Go Here For Free Instant Access:

www.PotentialRise.com

Legal Notice

Disclaimer Notice

the author and publisher reserve the right to alter and update the information contained herein on the new conditions whenever they see applicable.

Table Of Contents

Introduction

I want to thank you and congratulate you for purchasing the book, *"Ultimate Bitcoin For Beginners Guide! Bitcoin- Be Part Of The Currency Revolution And Understand Bitcoin Market Basics, Mining, Trading, Cryptocurrency, And More!"*

This "Bitcoin" book contains proven steps and strategies on how to be an expert in the bitcoin network.

BitCoin is becoming a very popular and practical method of earning money in the digital world. Today, where everything can be done online, using a digital currency that is decentralized and has purchasing power and monetary value can be an extremely feasible option to purchase goods and earn money at the same time without having to shell out cold cash.

There are three ways to earn money with BitCoins. First, you can earn by mining bitcoins, then you can do some buying and selling of goods using bitcoins and third, by trading bitcoins on an exchange.

This book also seeks to provide information regarding these details:

- Bitcoin history
- Bitcoin market basics
- Digital currency
- How to earn money by bitcoin trading
- Storing bitcoins safely
- Gold and silver investment
- Mining bitcoins
- Why bitcoin is important

- Beginner mistakes that should be avoided
- Exchange rates of bitcoins

Thanks again for purchasing this book, I hope you enjoy it!

Chapter 1: An Overview On The History Of Bitcoins

Satoshi Nakamoto was the software developer who proposed the use of bitcoins as a payment method. This system was generated with the intention of producing an electronic currency that can be transferred almost instantly with minimal fees for every transaction and one that is autonomous from any central supervision.

A person cannot mix out indefinite bitcoins. The bitcoin protocol states that there will only be twenty-one million bitcoins to be produced by the miners. These bitcoins will then be subdivided into smaller bits. The smallest bit is called 'satoshi' named after the bitcoin founder and the divisible amount is one hundred millionth of a bitcoin.

Bitcoin currency is based on mathematical formulas unlike our conventional currency that is based on gold and silver. Mathematics is used to generate or 'mine' bitcoins. The software programs containing these mathematical formulas are made available to everyone. This means that anyone can access these formulas to ensure that it serves its purpose.

There are three ways to earn money with BitCoins. First, you can earn by mining bitcoins, then you can do some buying and selling of goods using bitcoins and third, by trading bitcoins on an exchange.

All these methods will be discussed further in details as you move along the chapters of this book. Here, you can find the answers to your questions concerning bitcoins and the role it plays in the digital market. Even a beginner can definitely earn good money using bitcoins and this book seeks to help beginners discover the secrets within the bitcoin network.

This book will also provide tips on how to sell bitcoins, how to buy bitcoins, how to store them and how to earn money using the three given methods earlier. Bitcoin transactions will also be explained further for better understanding which is very important to all beginners. Furthermore, readers will find interesting bits of information regarding the goods and services that can be purchased through bitcoins.

Chapter 2: Basics Of The Bitcoin Market

Transactions governing bitcoins are sent to and from bitcoin wallets electronically and signatures are signed digitally for security. The history of transactions can be traced to where the bitcoins were first created and everyone within the bitcoin network knows how the transaction goes. If you are a speculator, you can hold on to your bitcoins and wait for the prices to go up but then again the point of using bitcoins is to spend it on goods and services.

So when you spend your bitcoins, how are you supposed to go through the transactions?

Bitcoins do not exist, only records of transactions:

The interesting part about bitcoins is that, they don't exist. If we are to look inside a certain bitcoin address, we will not be able to see any digital bitcoins inside it. When we check our conventional bank account, we will at least be able to see how much our dollars or Euros have grown in our account. With bitcoins, we can only see records of transactions from one address to another with decreasing or increasing balances. If you ever want to compute for the balance of a particular bitcoin address, that will not be possible unless you reconstruct the entire block chain and compute it.

During transactions, there will be three bits of important information recorded:

- Input: This information contains the bitcoin address used to send the bitcoins to another address.
- Amount: This refers to the amount of bitcoins sent to a particular bitcoin address
- Output: This information contains the bitcoin address of the recipient

How are bitcoins sent?

Each participant within the bitcoin network needs a private key and a bitcoin address. A private key refers to the sequence of numbers and letters which is kept personal and highly confidential. This is like a pass code or a PIN to your bank account. The bitcoin address on the other hand, is available to the public and is quite similar to your conventional bank account. The only difference is that, bitcoin address can be set-up without any hassles and requirements unlike the bank account.

Here's a typical scenario: Person A wants to send Person B some bitcoins. Person A then uses his private key to compose a message including the source of transaction, amount and the recipient's bitcoin address and signs it. Person A sends the bitcoins from his bitcoin wallet to a larger bitcoin network and the miners will then verify if the transaction is legitimate or not. Once verified the miners will place the transaction into a block and solves it eventually. The transaction usually lasts up to 10 minutes as the 'miners' process the data. For low value transactions, merchants process requests right away but for more important online transactions for example, it is expected to take a few minutes before one can take advantage of the services paid for or download the digital goods.

If in case the amount of input and output does not match, bitcoin network will create two separate transactions. For example: If person A want to send 2.5 bitcoins to Person B, and there is no exact amount inside person A's bitcoin address, then Person A uses the 3 bitcoin transaction and sends it to person B with the specific amount of 2.5. The network will then create a separate bitcoin address to hold person A's change of 0.5.

Transaction fees:

There is a corresponding transaction fee sometimes but not for every transaction. There are different factors affecting transaction fees and there are also some wallets that let you set manual transaction fees as you deemed proper. Any change not returned to the recipient or any transaction not picked up by the receiver is already considered a fee. The bitcoin will be given to the miner who will be lucky enough to solve it as a reward.

As of the moment there are no receipts given for every transaction.

Chapter 3: Understanding Digital Currency

BitCoin is held and created electronically and functions like a digital currency. No one can control the use and circulation of bitcoins. They are not printed like the normal currency we have today. Bitcoins are generated and produced globally by hundreds or thousands of people who know how to manipulate computers with the use of applications and software that can solve problems mathematically. This category of electronic money is otherwise known as cryptocurrency.

Just like ordinary currency like Euros and dollars, bitcoins are utilized to purchase goods electronically. Bitcoins can also be traded through digital means just like our conventional currencies. What makes it different from our ordinary currency is that, bitcoins are decentralized. It is normal that central banks control the currency of a certain country and in that respect; conventional money is centralized and controlled. Bitcoins on the other hand, is controlled by no one. There is no organization or institution that can control the network of bitcoins. This means that large banks cannot manipulate the people's money within the bitcoin network.

No one prints it as well because this type of currency is not controlled by any bank. This means that banks cannot impose any rules within the bitcoin network and it is also not accountable to the population. Conventional currency is produced, printed and circulated by the central bank of each country to cover national debt and this in a way can reduce or increase the value of the currency. The bitcoin network is different. It is digitally produced by people who join the community or the network. This network is distributed and using powerful computing device or software, bitcoins are 'mined'. Transactions made using this digital currency are processed within the bitcoin network making it an effective payment method.

Satoshi Nakamoto was the software developer who proposed the use of bitcoins as a payment method. This system was generated with the intention of producing an electronic currency that can be transferred almost instantly with minimal fees for every transaction and one that is autonomous from any central supervision.

Chapter 4: Tips On Becoming Rich By Buying/Trading Bitcoins

Another way to earn money through bitcoins is to buy them. Now the question is how can you buy bitcoins? Well, there are two ways to buy bitcoins. First is through exchange or trading and the second way is to buy them directly from people. Payment method can be done through credit/debit cards, cash or wire transfer and for some; you can also pay with the same cryptocurrency. Credit card payment or payment through PayPal is still not popular though because bitcoins transaction is mainly electronic. It is not easy to prove that there is an actual transfer of goods between two individuals and transactions can be reversed easily with a phone call to the card company.

So here are the things that you need to do in buying bitcoins:

1. **A bitcoin wallet is basic**: Before buying bitcoins, you need to provide yourself with a bitcoin wallet. It is similar to our conventional bank account. You can either store it using the web services or on your computer hard drive. Make sure to employ good security services against hackers for your web-based wallet. If you store it locally, it is better if you always back-up your files in case your drive becomes corrupted.

2. **Online wallets or exchanges**: If you plan to engage in regular speculation and trading, the best option for you is to have a wallet or exchange. It is recommended if you do not mind long procedures of identification and if you have no need of anonymity. Most countries require everyone to meet the requirements of Anti-money laundering and know your Customer principles. Some of the largest trading exchanges are: BTC-e, China's BTC, OKCoin and Huobi and the US Bitstamp and Kraken.

After the account set-up, you need to link your new exchange account and the existing bank account. Then you can move your funds from one account to the other through wire transfer. A fee is usually required to do that and some exchanges also permit personal deposit through their human teller. International transfer usually entails higher fees and long delays and some exchanges require bank transactions from that particular country only.

Although exchanges are one of the best options in buying bitcoins, it is important to note that there is no account insurance once the exchange goes bankrupt or is robbed by the hackers. This is because they are not regulated as most banks are. Take note that bitcoins are not officially recognized as a currency in most parts of the world so in case of theft and security issues, your money is not guaranteed safe. It is a must to ensure that your bank is bitcoin-friendly as there are banks that refuse to process transfers when bitcoins are concerned.

3. **Over-the-Counter Trades/Face to Face:** The OTC or FTF trade is the best option if you want to remain anonymous and if you want to avoid bank hassles. It is also recommended if you live in the city because it is easier to buy bitcoins from a local seller. You can visit LocalBitcoins site for this kind of transactions. Protection is also provided especially for bigger and more important transactions. It is better to meet in public place as it is safer and make sure that you always have access to your bitcoin wallet and Internet connection so you can confirm the transaction.

If in case you feel uncomfortable in meeting face to face, check your area if there is a group meeting at meetup.com. There is also some place in the big cities where bitcoin members meet through events called 'satoshi squares' where you can just walk-in, look around, buy bitcoins and leave. Group meetings are generally safer but you will not be able to enjoy total anonymity.

4. **Investment Trust**: There is a trust that exclusively invests in bitcoins and this is the BIT or Bitcoin Investment Trust. This is a good option if you do not prefer to store large quantity of bitcoins and buy. BIT utilizes a modern and high-tech protocol to safely store bitcoins for their shareholders or investors.

Chapter 5: Bitcoin Investment

With the growing popularity of the bitcoin network, more and more merchants start to accept bitcoin currency as a form of payment for goods and services sold online and in physical stores. Before, it is quite difficult and almost impossible to find a merchant that accepts bitcoins but today, even big international companies recognize bitcoin currency as a form of payment system. Although it is not yet globally recognized legally, bitcoin currency has shaped the digital world we have today.

So what can you buy with Bitcoins?

1. **Physical goods using e-commerce sites**: Computers and other electronic gadgets can be bought using bitcoins through online commerce sites. Dell is in partnership with a website known as Coinbase announcing that it is now accepting bitcoin as a mode of payment. Overstock, a major retailer is the first to accept bitcoin that offers electronics, jewellery and furniture. Although the prices are in dollars, the option for BTC on the checkout page is available to bitcoin users. As of today, bitcoin purchases are limited to US bitcoin users but this is definitely going to change in the near future.

The first bitcoin ATM in Scotland was also launched in May by a company named CeX as it initiated its bitcoin-only payment system. You can also buy flowers using bitcoins through 1-800-Flowers.com, which is a New York-based gift and flower shop in partnership with Coinbase.

Other e-commerce sites that accept bitcoin are: Bitcoinshop.us which offers products like watches and air conditioners and ships to people within the United States; Air Baltic, which is a Latvian airline also started accepting cryptocurrency mode of payment for basic class fares not including Taiwan, Malaysia, Vietnam, Russia, India, Japan, China, Iceland, Indonesia, Lebanon and Jordan. Travel booking websites also start to accept bitcoin sales on flights, hotel bookings to at least 200,000 hotels and railway Amtrak through their platforms. Even tickets for London shows and musicals can now be bought using bitcoins online. Coffee and pet grooming as well as Persian shoes and bags can also be purchased online using bitcoins.

2. **Physical stores**: The NBA franchise Sacramento Kings accepts bitcoins for payments for jerseys, caps, hotdogs, popcorns, beer and tickets. Bitcoin currency will be accepted online and in their home court Sleep Train Arena.

A large chain of jewelry in the US known as REEDS Jewelers also accepts bitcoin for payment. The California soccer club San Jose Earthquakes integrated bitcoin currency at their stadium starting May of this year 2014. Coinbase is the payment processor and bitcoins are used to purchase tickets and other merchandise sold in the stadium gift shop.

3. **Property and Hotels**: Cryptocurrency has also penetrated the travel and leisure communities with Expedia leading the innovation towards accepting bitcoins as a mode of payment for all bookings of hotels thereby making it the first prominent travel and leisure company to accept cryptocurrency. Expedia flight bookings will follow suit if everything goes well with the initiated program.

In Brooklyn New York, a famous hotel chain Holiday Inn Hotel also launched their pilot programme on cryptocurrency. Reservations made online, in person or by phone are payable with bitcoins. The first UK firm to also accept bitcoins as a form of payment was Cai-Capital.

4. **Restaurants and Bars**: If you are looking for some restaurants and bars that accept bitcoins as mode of payment, you can check Bitcoin.travel website and you will not be disappointed. The site offers numerous places like accommodations, beauty salons, bars, apartments and attractions around the world that accept bitcoins. The Pembury Tavern in London is one of the many places that accept bitcoin payments. In Sidney, Australia, the Old Fitzroy is a pub to visit and in Tokyo, The Pink Cow is one of the

best in town that accepts cryptocurrency payment.

In the Netherlands almost all of the businesses along the two canal-side streets found in the centre of the Hague started to collect bitcoins as a form of payment as well. These establishments include an art gallery and nine restaurants. The aforementioned canal-side streets Bierkade and Groenewegje have apparently changed to 'Bitcoin Boulevard'.

5. Services: When it comes to services, bitcoins can also be used for payment. An example of this is the DISH network which is one of the biggest American content providers based in Colorado with large number of subscribers reaching over fourteen million. The program for bitcoin payments has been scheduled to be effective in the third quarter of 2014 but no exact date has been given out yet. DISH network consists of more than 30,000 employees and the revenue reported as of last year reached 13.9 billion dollars. Once the bitcoin program is launched, DISH will be the largest company to accept bitcoin.

Chicago-sun times also started accepting bitcoins as payment in partnership with Coinbase for each subscription. This made Chicago-sun Times the first newspaper company to accept bitcoins as a mode of payment.

6. Education: Can you imagine using bitcoins to pay for your education? Yes it is possible. Treehouse, an interactive education specialist based in Florida started accepting bitcoins for payments on the web developments and designs subscription services. The aforementioned firm has 70,000 students to date and was able to raise 24.6 million dollars with support from 6 funding rounds.

OKCupid which is one of the most popular dating and matchmaking sites just started accepting bitcoin payments in April last year.

7. Technical and web services: It is not surprising to know that bitcoin network has been receiving a lot of support from the online community. Bitcoin functions electronically and participants are required to at least have sufficient technical knowledge and skills so it is quite expected that bitcoin has acquired numerous attention from online community services. Some hosting companies offer web services in exchange for some bitcoins.

Another popular website and platform is the WordPress. In exchange for a bitcoin, WordPress will give you an online blogging presence. Other web service credits for companies like Xboxlive, AirVPN, Spotify, PlayStation Network and Steam can be purchased through Bitcoin Codes online. For domain services, bitcoins can be paid directly through Namecheap. There are also several VPN providers that accept bitcoins only as mode of payment.

8. **Bullion Trade**: Since 2012, Amagi Metals started trading precious metals for bitcoins. This company sells bullion in exchange for bitcoins through their e-commerce site which can be accessed anywhere in the world. Amagi Metals believe bitcoins are excellent tools in the promotion of the growing interest in financial responsibility.

9. **Donations and Give-away**: If you have a heart for the less fortunate, you can donate your bitcoins to some charitable organizations that accept bitcoins. If you want to reward someone for a very appealing performance or comment, you can give-away your bitcoins as well. Some charitable organizations are: Sean's Outpost, which is a shelter for the homeless in Pensacola, Florida and the Sri Lanka Campaign for Peace and Justice which is a non-government organization focused on their campaign for reconciliation, human rights and justice in Sri Lanka.

Tipping using your bitcoins is also possible in reddit.

Chapter 6: Tips On Storing Bitcoins Safely

Bitcoins are stored in bitcoin wallets. This is basic and the primary requirement before one can enter the bitcoin network and start with transactions. Now, just like the conventional currency, bitcoins need to be stored safely as well. Here are some tips on how to store bitcoins safely.

1.Wallet encryption: Just like any other online accounts, bitcoin wallets need to be secured with an encrypted password. Encryption makes access by the owner possible and easy but very difficult for other people. Malware makes it possible for your computer to be hacked by thieves as they can log keystrokes for finding out your password so it should be encrypted.

2. Wallet needs to be backed up: Wallet owners have their own private keys but sometimes keys could be misplaced or forgotten and so it is important that wallets should be backed up so you can at least have a copy of your private keys when needed. Backing up your wallet and storing it in different places makes it very secured from prying eyes especially when some transactions are accessible to public.

3. Cold storage wallets may be your best option: If you are very careful and reluctant to store your wallets through digital means, take it offline and use the "cold storage" option. This option makes it impossible for online hackers to steal your bitcoins as your wallet is not accessible online no matter what. Cold storage is very ideal for storing bigger bulks of bitcoin fortune. When you need to spend online, all you have to do is to transfer a fair bit of bitcoin to your addresses online and you can do transactions as normal as possible. Cold storage also saves your bitcoin fortune in case of computer problems or when your phone is lost.

Paper wallets can also be used if you are not comfortable in using digital wallets altogether.

Chapter 7: Importance Of Bitcoins

A person cannot mix out indefinite bitcoins. The bitcoin protocol states that there will only be twenty-one million bitcoins to be produced by the miners. These bitcoins will then be subdivided into smaller bits. The smallest bit is called 'satoshi' named after the bitcoin founder and the divisible amount is one hundred millionth of a bitcoin.

Bitcoin currency is based on mathematical formulas unlike our conventional currency that is based on gold and silver. Mathematics is used to generate or 'mine'bitcoins. The software programs containing these mathematical formulas are made available to everyone. This means that anyone can access these formulas to ensure that it serves its purpose.

Important characteristics of Bitcoins:

These are some significant characteristics or features of bitcoins that separate them from conventional currency we have today.

1. **Bitcoins are not centralized**: No central authority can control the bitcoin network. Even a large bank cannot trifle the fiscal regulations and procedures governing the bitcoin network. All machines used in mining and processing bitcoins and other transactions work together and compose a fraction of the bitcoin network. This means that even if a fraction of the network goes offline, the money will still flow.

2. **The set-up is quick and easy:** A person who wants to join the bitcoin network can set-up the bitcoin address in seconds. Unlike conventional banks where one has to go through long queues of people just to open an account. There are no restrictions or other unnecessary requirements and documents to be submitted to the bitcoin network and there are no fees to be paid as well.

3. **Privacy or anonymity**: Bitcoin users enjoy the privilege of holding multiple addresses which are not connected to other personal information such as addresses and names.

4. **Transparent**: Your identity may be anonymous to the network and the public but the transactions you make and the number of bitcoins stored in your address are definitely recorded. The block chain records everything. The public will be able to see all the activities in the given bitcoin address but they will not be able to know that the address is yours for example. Some users utilize different bitcoin addresses so they can avoid putting all the bitcoins in just one address. That way they can enjoy the benefits of being anonymous...

5. **Minimal transaction fees**: Bitcoin does not charge international transfers unlike the banks we have for conventional currencies.

6. **Procedures are quick and almost instant**: When you have to send money internationally, there are times you have to wait for a few days before the bank can process the transaction and transfer it to the other account. With bitcoin network, your money is transferred anywhere in just a matter of a few minutes or almost in an instant depending on the location. Transactions are very quick.

7. **Bitcoins cannot be repudiated**: One cannot reclaim his bitcoins once they are sent. They can only get it back when the recipient sends it back to the sender otherwise it is gone for good.

Chapter 8: Secret Tips On Mining Bitcoins

One way to earn good money is by mining bitcoins. So how does bitcoin mining works?

Conventional money is produced and generated by the central banks and people earn it in so many ways. If the government needs more money they just print more money. This system is different than the bitcoin network. Bitcoins are discovered using computer software that contains mathematical formulas. Users who participate in this network 'mine' for bitcoins by contending each other.

Every transaction within the bitcoin network is recorded. When people send bitcoins to each other, the general ledger will trace it and record it to keep track of every transaction. These transactions are collected within a given period of time and compiled in a list called the 'block'. The confirmation of each transactions will go to the 'miners' and they will document them in the GL.

The long list of blocks composes the block chain or the general ledger. Here, all transactions are transparent so everyone can see the activities that take place in every bitcoin addresses. New blocks created are added to the block chain and updates will be given to everyone who participates in the network to maintain transparency of transactions.

The 'miners' ensure that the block chain remains uncorrupted and intact. This is the reason why the GL or the block chain is trusted by everyone inside the network.

As each block is produced or collected, the 'miners' take all the information and they turn it into something else by applying mathematical formulas into it. The processed product is known as the 'hash' and it is composed of random letters and numbers. The 'hash' is stored at the end of the block chain along with the block.

It is important to note that each 'hash' is unique from each other. It may be easy to produce out of collected blocks but without knowledge of the mathematical formulas, it is not possible to know what the data is all about. Changing just one character in a bitcoin block will definitely change its 'hash' totally.

The 'hash' that miners add to the block functions like a wax seal. Each 'hash' is produced using the 'hash' of the former block. This way, the chain of blocks are ensured to be legitimate and once it's tampered, the hash of the succeeding blocks will all be changed completely creating a chaotic domino effect. All the blocks with changed 'hash' will then be tagged as fake so tampering is very noticeable.

Coin competition:

To avoid tampering of blocks, 'miners' seal off each block using mathematical formulas. 'Miners' will get a reward of 25 bitcoins for every successful 'hash' created and then the block chain will be updated for everyone to know. Old 'hash' will not be accepted so each 'miner' has to abide with the bitcoin protocol known as 'proof of work'. In order for them to create a different 'hash' every time, 'miners' need to use 'nonce' which is a random piece of data. Oftentimes, 'nonce' does not work and so 'miners' has to try many times to find out a 'nonce' that work. Once they are able to discover a 'nonce' that work then they are able to create a successful hash and they earn 25 bitcoins as a reward.

Chapter 9: Mistakes To Avoid By Beginners

As a beginner, there are things that you have to be aware of when you enter the bitcoin network. This is very important so that you will know what to expect and avoid untoward incidents. Here are the common problems that you have to be careful of as a beginner...

1. As time increases, so is the difficulty of your currency level: Your tools and equipments will reduce mining shares and earning coins overtime. When you enter the bitcoin protocol you have to invest on the best equipment that you can afford first so that your chances of being able to mine longer than your counterparts are greater. Long-term profitability is also relevant to the volatility of the currency that you mine. Just like the stock market, when prices suddenly drop, there will only be two options for you, you can either wait until the value of your bitcoins increases or you can sell them to other participants. If you choose to wait longer, you have to compensate for the cost of electricity and expenditures by longer mining...

2. Keep calm and be cool: Bitcoin mining is not easy so expect that you will be under so much stress as you compete with other participants in the bitcoin network. As temperature increases, the difficulty of mining decreases so it is always important to keep your tools and equipment cool and the ventilation is sufficient. Beer crates sometimes are used by mining rig builders because air flow is maximized other than using cases of PC. A desktop fan is enough to keep your computer and other kits cool.

3. Anticipate power failures: If you buy a cheap PSU in building a Do-it-yourself mining rig, it will not be a practical and smart move. The Power supply should be well thought of and should be stable and reliable because instability in power supply can definitely affect the performance negatively. It can even result to a system crash so invest in a good quality unit always to avoid downtime.

Tips for avoiding downtime:

- Un-interruptible power supply or UPS is recommended so that the miner will not be affected in case of electricity supply cuts.
- Buy the best quality power supply that is within your budget
- Always think that you are losing money when your hardware isn't mining
- Change the setting of your mining equipment and have it configured to launch mining session during start-up automatically. Some computers and DIY mining rigs are designed that way so when the electricity is cut and the equipment reboots, mining will start again automatically.

4. Costs in mining that you might not know about: The ongoing electricity consumption and the rig are some of the costs you have to be aware of when mining. There are other extra expenditures though:

a. Customs and delivery: When you want something delivered at your doorstep from another country like the Jalapeno ASIC miner, you are surely required to pay a significant amount of Euros or dollars to the customs and delivery costs. Check out the costs first before you plan on importing any important item.

b. Accessories: When you use computers, you will certainly need some accessories at some point like adapters or cable wires. SO make sure to plan ahead on what you really need and invest on good quality always.

c. Cooling costs: Computers require good ventilation and cooling system so apart from your electric bill, you also have to deal with air-conditioning costs or fan costs.

Chapter 10: Tips On Reading Bitcoin Exchange Rates

Miners and bitcoin network participants should know how exchanging rates in the bitcoin industry works. It is not like the conventional currency we use because in the bitcoin industry, there are only 2 currencies you have to deal with. The two most common and widely mined currencies are Sha-256 and the Scrypt.

In order to know how exchange rates to conventional currency work, miners and bitcoin network participants need to know a few reliable websites that can be used for calculating profitability. Parameters such as hash rate, equipment costs, power supply consumption, and the ongoing price of your bitcoin need to be entered on the profitability calculators so you would know how long will it take for your investment to be paid back.

Some websites made some tests using the profitability calculators of two mining systems. The one mentioned above was used in computing for the GPU Scrypt mining rig and for Sha0256 currency ASIC miner the one from the Butterfly Lab in the UK was used. Considering the cost of electricity consumption per kilowatt hour, the recommendations and profits presented by the following sites are as follows:

Bitcoin specific calculators:

Genesis block: 1.20 dollars a day for every bitcoin

Bitcoinx: 1.42 dollars a day

Multi-currency calculators:

Coinwarz:

Sha-256: 1.14 dollars a day

Scrypt: 39.13 per day per Dogecoin

Dustcoin:

Sha-256: 1.43 dollars a day per Freicoin

Scrypt: 31.05 dollars a day per Dogecoin

Conclusion

Thank you again for purchasing this book on the *"Ultimate Bitcoin for Beginners Guide! Bitcoin- Be Part Of The Currency Revolution And Understand Bitcoin Market Basics, Mining, Trading, Cryptocurrency, And More!"*

I am extremely excited to pass this information along to you, and I am so happy that you now have read and can hopefully implement these strategies going forward.

I hope this book was able to help you understand the basic bitcoin market protocol and how to go about the bitcoin network transactions.

The next step is to get started using this information and to hopefully live a successful and very promising bitcoin-influenced life!

Please don't be someone who just reads this information and doesn't apply it, the strategies in this book will only benefit you if you use them!

If you know of anyone else that could benefit from the information presented here please inform them of this book.

Finally, if you enjoyed this book and feel it has added value to your life in any way, please take the time to share your thoughts and post a review on Amazon. It'd be greatly appreciated!

Thank you and good luck!

Preview Of:

<u>How To Be Rich</u>

Discover How To Be Rich Using Money Rules Of The Rich To Make Money, Gain Passive Income, Be Debt Free, And Financially Free In 6 Simple Steps!

Introduction

I want to thank you and congratulate you for purchasing the book, *"How To Be Rich - Discover How To Be Rich Using Money Rules Of The Rich To Make Money, Gain Passive Income, Be Debt Free, And Financially Free In 6 Simple Steps!"*.

This book contains proven steps and strategies on how to think and operate your financial affairs like the wealthy.

Have you ever wondered how you can take two people working the same job with the same salary and one seems to always have money while the other seems to always be broke? Or have you ever wondered how a self made millionaire is able to rise out of the lower level of society while another seems to be trapped?

Well, if you have ever contemplated on these things, then you are in the right place! There is a process to wealth creation, some may call it a formula, but it is undoubtedly not the result of luck. If you want to get from A-Z, if you want to get to the top of the mountain, you have to have a roadmap. This is your roadmap.

Sometimes the hardest thing to do is to start! Unfortunately this is also the most important part. If you never start, you will never accomplish anything in life, let alone major ambitions. Please don't delay any longer! Stop putting your future on hold, and begin at once towards the amazing life you were born to live and should already be enjoying! I wish you the best of luck in this endeavor, and hope you will choose this book and its principles to be a part of your exciting accent to the top!

Thanks again for purchasing this book, I hope you enjoy it!

Chapter 1 - Living Within 80% Or Less Of Your Income

The fact that you have an income doesn't mean that you need to spend all those income as you please. Sure you can – but you should not if you want to become rich. Many people believe that they work to live and vice versa, thus making them slaves of the vicious cycle of "working for a living". This need not happen to you, and it certainly would not if you follow the rules on accumulating wealth.

The first thing that you need to remember is that you should live within 80% or less of your income. Yes, you heard it right! You cannot go all out with your pay check if you want to become rich. The next question would be: what would you do with your money?

As a basic rule, you need some part of your income to be able to afford your basic needs, i.e. water, food, clothes, electricity etc. You simply have to, or you will not survive. The good news is that there is no problem with spending on them so long as you put a limit on how much you need to spend. You see, being rich does not mean that you have to deprive yourself of the things you need. After all, you have worked hard for that money and you deserve to have a piece of it.

In spending the money you have earned, make sure that you don't go beyond the allowable limit which is 80%. Remember that the 80% should answer for all the things you need to buy or pay for. This goes to tell that you should not have expenses beyond the 80% limit. If you are earning $1200 per month, make sure that your way of living can be sustained by $960 per month and no more. This should cover your food, water and electric bills, rent (if any), transportation costs, and other expenses. If the $960 is not enough for you to last a month, you need to cut off on expenses that you don't need i.e. movie 3x/month, VIP golf membership dues, etc. In simple words, cut those expenses that would go beyond your limit.

You may ask, "Why do I need to do that when the entire $1200 can cover all that?" The answer is simple – because you want to be rich. How does spending on 80% of your income make you rich? Here's how:

- It puts a limit on spending

Since you have a ceiling on your allowable expenses, it automatically shuts off further spending on your part. The fact that you are only allowed to spend on a certain extent makes you think about *not spending* the rest, hence a spending limit you would not otherwise have.

- It helps you to determine which ones you really need

People often buy things they don't really need, resulting both wasted time and money. But because you are only allowed to spend 80% of your income, you are now forced to determine which ones are among the priority expenses. As such, you will have to dispense with the things you don't really need to prevent wasted resources and focus on the more important things that you need in your life.

- It allows you to have spare money

Spare money is very important in maintaining one's financial stability. Life is very uncertain and more often than not, people won't really have time to prepare for the next expenses to come. Saving 20% of your income helps you to gain some leverage financially, especially in times of need.

- It hones your skill of managing your finances

Some say that people show their ability and discipline best when confronted with boundaries or limitations. Having an

80% spending limit tests your skill in managing your finances, which in turn could hone you to become a better and wiser spender in the long run.

Now that you know what to do with 80% of your income, the next thing that you have to know is what to do with the remaining 20%. What does that 20% represent? How does that 20% make a difference in your way of life?

The remaining 20% of your income represents your savings. It is the spare money that you can count on in times of need, thus giving you some financial security and room for other necessary expenses. It gives you more power financially and more security psychologically because you won't be threatened by life events you never planned or in any way expected. In other words, you would be more economically stable. Such amount can make a huge difference between financial uncertainty and financial stability. Of course you wouldn't want to be on the bad side, would you?

However, do not be too complacent with the fact that you have saved at least 20% of your income in a storage box. The fact is, the way you manage that 20% savings is as important as the way you manage the 80% of your income. If you want to be rich, there is no question that you should manage both WISELY. But exactly how can you do that?

Here are where your savings should go:

- Business Fund

  As you will learn later on, having a business investment is very important in creating wealth. Surely, you would need a capital from which you would build your business. Save a business fund for this goal as early as today so that you will have enough money when the time comes that you are ready to venture into the business world.

- Charity Fund

Set aside being filthy rich – what you need to be is a rich man with a heart. As a person, you need to help people in need whether they are complete strangers or the closest of your friends. As the law of karma always says, helping is an investment in itself. Surely, you want to reap the fruits of your good deeds later on!

- Emergency Fund

  No one knows for sure what will happen next. The future is uncertain and the only way for you to be prepared for what might come is to make sure that your weapons are ready. Have an emergency fund that you can count on anytime and in any event so you won't be caught off guard!

- Car Fund

  A means of transportation is also very essential in building your wealth. In order to be rich, you need to have the ability to move around places as you deal with transactions. This could only be attained by having a reliable means of transport – a car.

  This car fund is not only to be used to purchase a car (if you don't have one yet); it should also be a fund ready to answer for car repairs and improvements.

- Miscellaneous Fund

  Expenses which cannot be classified into a specified group should be covered under miscellaneous fund. This is where you should get the money to finance unexpected, little costs you haven't expected in your budget. This gives you a little leeway for spending on things that you need but failed to account for in your budget.

- Pleasure Fund

>   Truth be told, pleasure is a basic human need. Whether it is as grand as having a world cruise or a simple movie per week agenda, your pleasure has to be incorporated in your life.
>
>   All people have their own choices when it comes to what gives them pleasure, some more costly than others. The reason why you need to have a fund to answer for your pleasure expenses is so that you will never have to choose or compromise between necessities and pleasure. You can have both and still be rich! You might think that these funds cannot be covered by the 20% fund alone, and you're correct about that to an extent. But the thing is, these are some of the funds that you can utilize in times of need.

The manner on which you want to distribute the savings is up to you; you may divide the 20% equally or depending on your priorities. If you badly want a car, you may allot more to your car fund that in any other funds. You see, there is no hard and fast rule when it comes to your savings so long as you have these important fund classifications with you. All of these accounts are important for you to attain the financial stability you're aiming for.

To better utilize these funds, you can go to a reliable credit union where you can set up 6 accounts representing each fund. Aside from having them take care of your accounts of you, you can also be sure that you won't be able to spend your money on impulse as when you have the money on hand.

If you don't find (or want) a credit union to handle your savings, you can definitely just use an envelope to separate these funds under one account. Either way, you accomplish your goal of savings utilization by putting up different funds.

Thanks for Previewing My Exciting Book Entitled:

"How To Be Rich: Discover How To Be Rich Using Money Rules Of The Rich To Make Money, Gain Passive Income, Be Debt Free, And Financially Free In 6 Simple Steps!"

To purchase this book, simply go to the Amazon Kindle store and simply search:

"HOW TO BE RICH"

Then just scroll down until you see my book. You will know it is mine because you will see my name "James Harper" underneath the title.

Alternatively, you can visit my author page on Amazon to see this book and other work I have done. Thanks so much, and please don't forget your free bonuses

DON'T LEAVE YET! - CHECK OUT YOUR FREE BONUSES BELOW!

Free Bonus Offer: Get Free Access To The PotentialRise.com VIP Newsletter!

Once you enter your email address you will immediately get free access to this awesome newsletter!

But wait, right now if you join now for free you will also get free access to the "LIMITLESS ENERGY" free EBook!

To claim both your FREE VIP NEWSLETTER MEMBERSHIP and your FREE BONUS Ebook on LIMITLESS ENERGY!

Just Go To:

www.PotentialRise.com